9/18

# I WANT TO DRAW DOGS

**FRANK FELICE**

**PowerKiDS** press

New York

Published in 2019 by The Rosen Publishing Group, Inc.
29 East 21st Street, New York, NY 10010

Copyright 2001; reprint 2019

Editor: Greg Roza
Book Design: Tanya Dellaccio

Photo Credits: Front Cover, back cover, pp. 1, 3–24 Chiociolla/Shutterstock.com; Cover sssss1gmel/iStock; p. 5 (pencil and sharpener) KET-SMM/Shutterstock.com; p. 5 (boy) Anna Grigorjeva/Shutterstock.com; p. 6 miroslav chytil/Shutterstock.com; p. 8 Anna Goroshinikova/Shutterstock.com; pp. 10, 18 Grigorita Ko/Shutterstock.com; p. 12 Elena Lar/Shutterstock.com; p. 14 Lenkadan/Shutterstock.com; p. 16 Alexey Androsov/Shutterstock.com; p. 20 Natalia Fedosova/Shutterstock.com.

Cataloging-in-Publication Data

Names: Felice, Frank.
Title: I want to draw dogs / Frank Felice.
Description: New York : PowerKids Press, 2019. | Series: Learn to draw! | Includes glossary and index.
Identifiers: LCCN ISBN 9781508167884 (pbk.) | ISBN 9781508167860 (library bound) | ISBN 9781508167891 (6 pack)
Subjects: LCSH: Dogs in art–Juvenile literature. | Drawing–Technique–Juvenile literature.
Classification: LCC NC783.8.D64 F45 2019 | DDC 743.6'9772–dc23

Manufactured in the United States of America

CPSIA Compliance Information: Batch CS18PK: For Further Information contact Rosen Publishing, New York, New York at 1-800-237-9932

# CONTENTS

# DOG DRAWING

Have you ever wanted to have a pet dog? Dogs are called man's best friend for a reason, and there are many different kinds. In this book you'll be introduced to seven different **breeds** of dogs, plus one wolf. Even though most dogs look very different from one another, it is important to remember that many dogs come for the same **ancestor**: the wolf. In the first drawing, you will draw the gray wolf. The dogs of today share many **traits** with the wild gray wolf. As you continue to learn how to draw new breeds of dogs, you'll notice how they are all similar to the gray wolf.

Just like their wolf ancestors, dogs all have different kinds of fur. Some fur is long and soft, while other fur is short and stiff. You will learn how to draw both kinds of fur. The more you draw, the better you will get at it. Before you start, make sure you find a quiet and well-lit space where you can draw your new dog friends.

Once you've got your sketch pad, pencil, pencil sharpener, and eraser ready, you can start drawing some dogs.

# DRAWING THE GRAY WOLF

Before the dog, there was the wild wolf. The gray wolf is known to have **evolved** about 300,000 years ago. Many traits of the gray wolf are still seen in dogs today. Two of these traits are being **loyal** and being great hunters. Researchers believe that the wolf was tamed by humans about 12,000 years ago.

Bones of this animal were found in the Beaverhead Mountains of Idaho, and also in Europe and Asia. The gray wolf could once be found all over the world. Unfortunately, people started hunting the gray wolf and damaging the lands where it lived. From the 1970s to the 2010s, gray wolves were protected in the United States.

**Gray wolves are still recovering from being heavily hunted by humans.**

**1** Begin by drawing three circles. Notice where they are placed on the page and their different sizes.

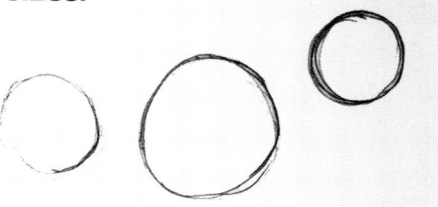

**2** Next, connect the circles to form the body of the gray wolf.

**3** Wonderful! Now draw the two shapes shown to form the legs of the gray wolf.

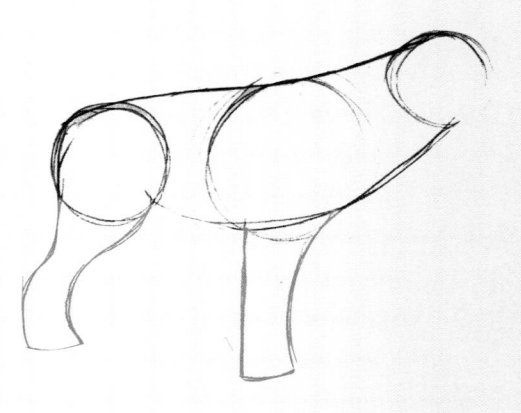

**4** Next, draw in the shape of the mouth in the front and the shape of the tail in the back..

**5** Are you beginning to see the gray wolf? Now let's add some detail to the head. Draw the ear, the eye, the nose, and the mouth.

**6** You're doing great! Now add lines as shown to complete legs. Erase extra lines. Shade mouth and ear. That's your first gray wolf!

# DRAWING THE GOLDEN RETRIEVER

Golden retrievers are well loved around the world. There are many great things about golden retrievers. They are gentle, fun-loving, loyal, and easy to train. They are also known for their beautiful golden coats.

Golden retrievers were first **developed** in Great Britain as hunting dogs. They are called retrievers because they like to hunt and to carry things in their mouths. Golden retrievers came to America from Europe in 1925. At first, they were used mostly as hunting dogs. Before long, they became popular house pets. Because they are easy to train, some golden retrievers are **service animals** for people with special needs.

**Countless families all over the world love their golden retrievers.**

**1** Begin by drawing three circles. Notice where they are placed on the page and their different sizes.

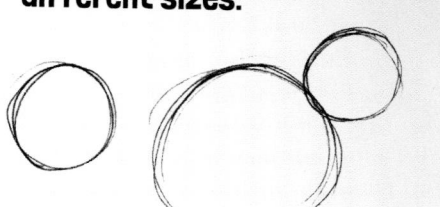

**2** Next, connect the circles to form the body of the golden retriever.

**3** Good job! Now draw a square shape for the mouth in the front. Draw the curved shape of the tail in the back.

**4** Draw the legs underneath the body by making four shapes that look kind of like rectangles with curved sections.

**5** You're doing great! Now let's draw in the face. Draw the eye, the nose, the mouth, and the ear.

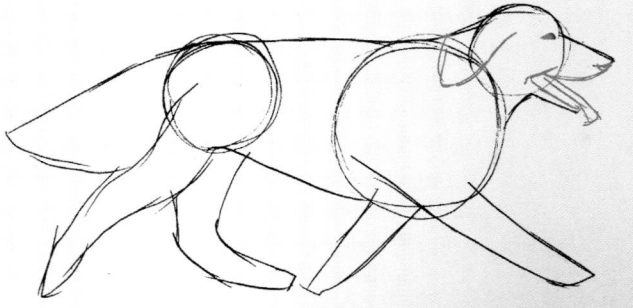

**6** Finish the drawing by erasing any extra lines. Try shading in your drawing. To make the fur look soft and wavy, shade line by line. Excellent! You drew a golden retriever!

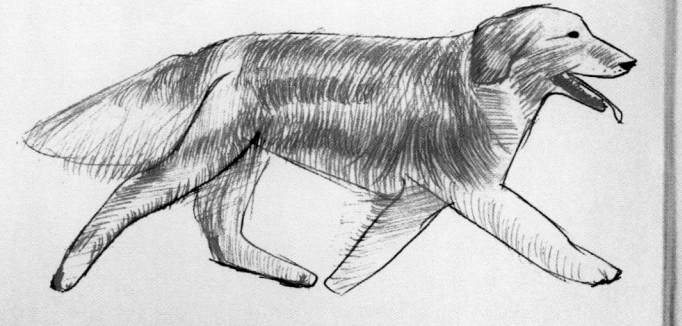

# DRAWING THE DALMATIAN

Dalmatians are very special dogs with a long history. They look different from other dogs because of their **unique** spotted coats. Dalmatians are born all white. As they grow, they develop dark spots. It is unknown exactly where Dalmatians are from. Some believe that they came from an area called Dalmatia in Eastern Europe, which is how they got their name.

One thing that is certain is that the Dalmatian became a very popular and useful dog. In England in the 1600s, for example, Dalmatians often helped out at firehouses. In those days, fire "trucks" were actually horse-drawn carriages. To help the firemen, a Dalmatian would run ahead of the carriage and bark to clear the way.

**Dalmatians are easy to recognize because of their beautiful black spots.**

**1** Begin by drawing three circles. Notice where they are placed on the page and their different sizes.

**2** Next, connect the circles to form the body of the Dalmatian.

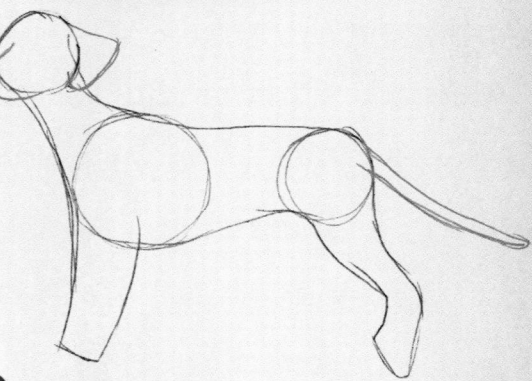

**3** Excellent! Now draw two shapes to form the front and back legs of the Dalmatian.

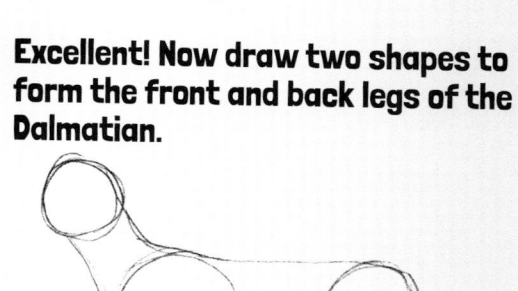

**4** Draw in the shapes of the ear and mouth in the front and the shape of the tail at back.

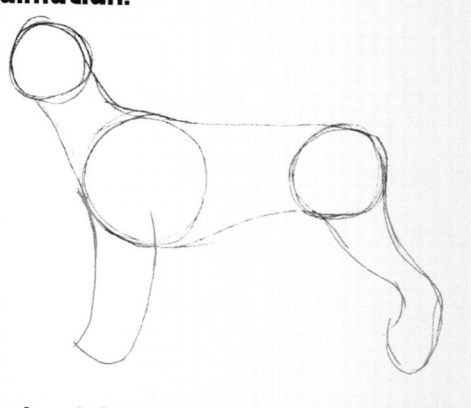

**5** You're doing great! Now draw in the legs by adding lines as shown in the leg shapes.

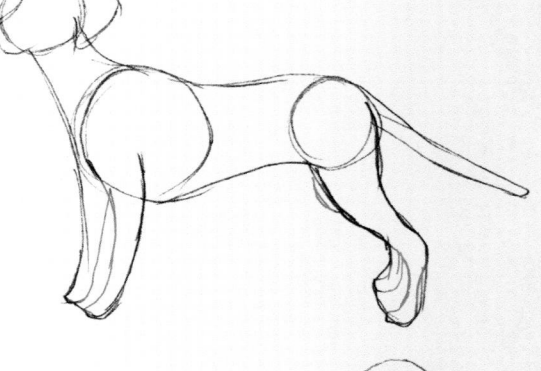

**6** Excellent! Now let's add the face. Draw the eyes, the nose, and the mouth.

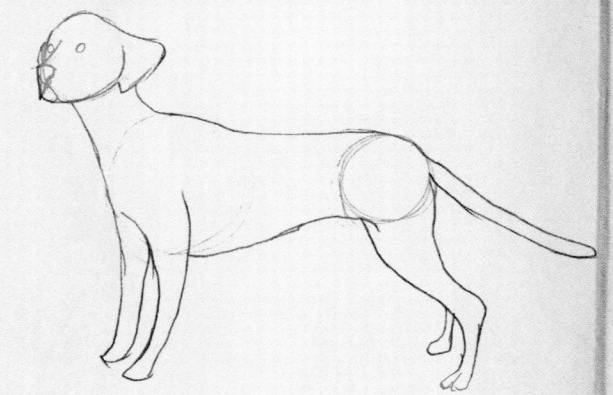

**7** Finish the drawing by erasing any extra lines and drawing in the spots. Good for you! You just drew a Dalmatian!

# DRAWING THE CHIHUAHUA

Chihuahuas have a very unique appearance. The breed is known for having a tiny body, an apple-shaped head, bright eyes, and big ears. The Chihuahua is one of the smallest types of dog. Commonly, Chihuahuas weigh between 3 and 6 pounds (1.4 and 2.7 kg). They can have long or short fur. You will be drawing a Chihuahua with short fur.

The Chihuahua gets its name from a state in Mexico. The breed is believed to come from a dog known as the Techichi, which can be traced back to ninth century Mexico. This dog is considered the start of the Chihuahua breed.

**Chihuahuas are known to pack a lot of energy in their tiny bodies.**

**1** Begin by drawing three circles. Notice where they are placed on the page and their different sizes.

**2** Connect the circles to form the body of the Chihuahua.

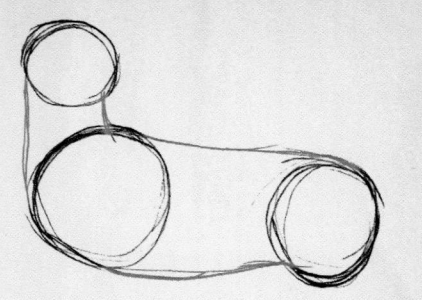

**3** Excellent! Now draw two shapes as shown to form the front and back legs of the Chihuahua

**4** Draw two triangles on the top circle for the ears. Draw the tail in the back.

**5** You're doing great! Now let's add the face. Draw the eyes, the nose, and the mouth. Draw a curved line to finish the back leg.

**6** Finish the drawing by erasing any extra lines. If you want, add some shading to your drawing. To make the fur look wavy and soft, shade line by line.

# DRAWING THE BOXER

Despite its name, the boxer does not really box. The breed got its name from the way it raises its paws when it plays or fights, like a human boxer. Standing 23 inches (58 cm) tall, the boxer is a very friendly and loyal dog.

Boxers are known for being hard-working and good with people. They have a great sense of smell and excellent hearing. Throughout history these qualities have been useful to their human companions. There are many stories of boxers helping people by **sniffing** out danger or protecting their homes.

**Because they like to protect their owners, boxers make great guard dogs.**

**1** Begin by drawing three circles. Notice where they are placed on the page and their different sizes.

**2** Next, connect the circles to form the body of the boxer.

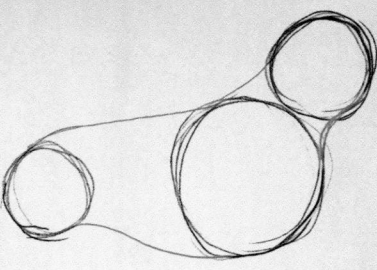

**3** Wonderful! Now draw two shapes to form the front and back legs of the boxer.

**4** Draw in the shape of the mouth. Add ears to the top circle.

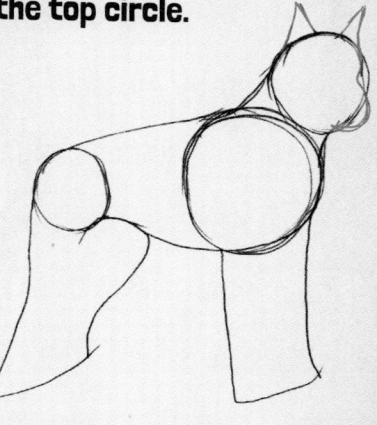

**5** You're doing great! Finish the legs by drawing the vertical and curved lines as shown.

**6** Excellent! Now let's add the face. Draw the eyes, nose, and mouth.

**7** Finish the drawing by erasing any extra lines. Shade in the eyes and nose and add on the tail. Great job!

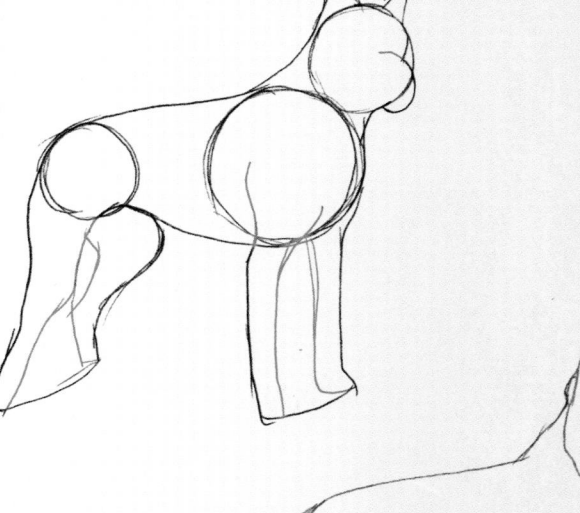

# DRAWING THE BEAGLE

Short and full of energy, beagles are happy dogs. They are happy to be with people, happy to help them, happy to be at home, and especially happy to hunt. The beagle's **personality** is a big reason why it is so popular. Beagles are playful, loyal, and smart.

Bred as hunting hounds, beagles are very good at sniffing out prey. A beagle can sniff out a rabbit hours after it is gone from sight. Because of their great sense of smell, beagles have been used as scent-detecting dogs at airports. Instead of bombs or drugs, many beagles are used to find food and plants that are being brought into a country illegally.

**Beagles are mainly led by their noses when they hunt and play.**

**1** Begin by drawing three circles. Notice where they are placed on the page and their different sizes.

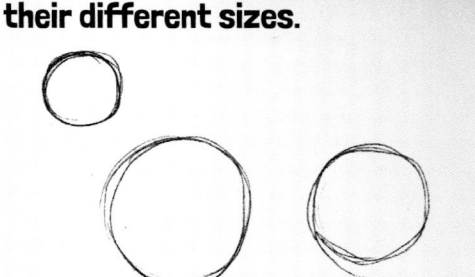

**2** Next, connect the circles to form the body of the beagle.

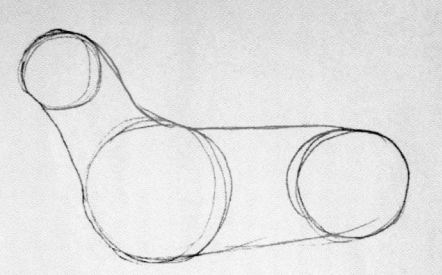

**3** Good job! Now draw two shapes as shown to form the front and back legs of the beagle.

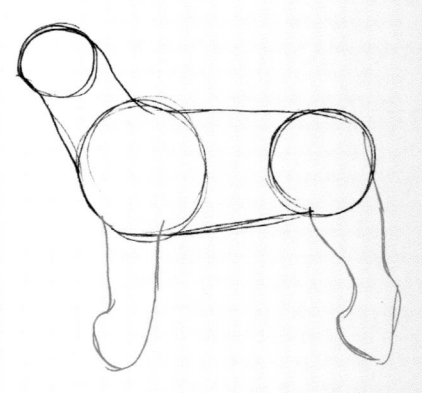

**4** Draw the mouth in the front and the tail in the back.

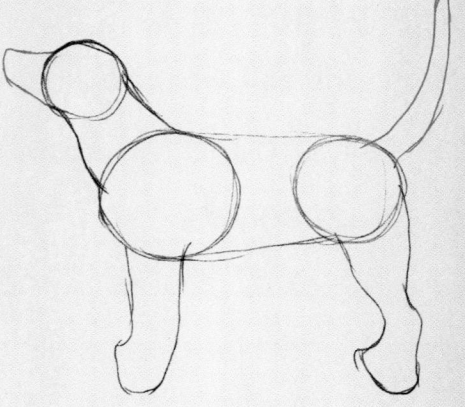

**5** You're doing great! Now finish the front and back legs by drawing in curved lines as shown.

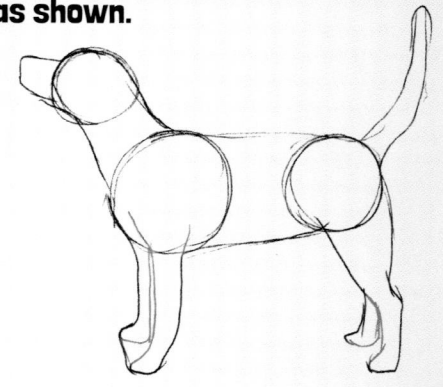

**6** Now draw in the face. Draw an eye, the nose, the mouth, and an ear.

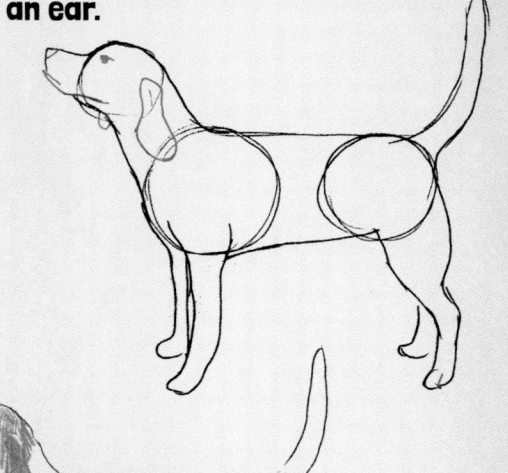

**7** Finish the drawing by erasing any extra lines. If you want, try shading in the markings of the beagle. To make the look of the wavy coat, shade line by line. Excellent! You just drew a beagle!

# DRAWING THE BASENJI

Coming from Central Africa, the basenji is known as the "barkless dog." It does not bark like other dogs. Instead, it makes unique **yodeling** and growling sounds. Basenjis have short fur and a curly tail. Basenjis clean themselves by licking their fur, especially around the face. This is very similar to the way cats clean themselves.

The word "basenji" means "bush thing" or "wild thing" in a native African language. The basenji was mostly used as a hunting dog in Africa. The have very good eyesight and a terrific sense of smell. While they are not used much for hunting today, they still are very active.

**Basenjis came to England in the 1930s and the United States about 50 years later.**

**1** Begin by drawing three circles. Notice where they are placed on the page and their different sizes.

**2** Next, connect the circles to form the body of the basenji.

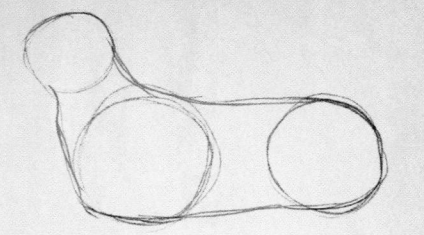

**3** Beautiful! Now draw two shapes to form the front and back legs of the basenji.

**4** Draw in the shape of the mouth in the front. Draw a circle for the curled tail in the back.

**5** You're doing great! Now draw two curved triangles to make the ears. Draw another small circle inside the circle you drew for the tail.

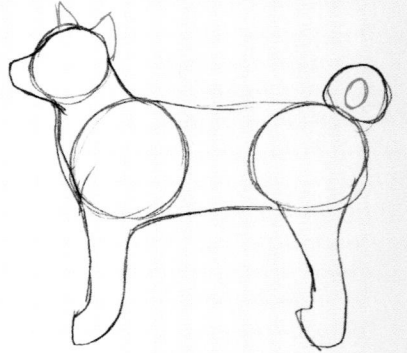

**6** Excellent! Now let's draw in the face. Draw an eye, the nose, and the mouth. Add lines to complete the legs.

**7** Finish the drawing by erasing any extra lines. Shade in the ears, an eye, the nose, and the tail. Great job!

# DRAWING THE SALUKI

Dating back to 2100 BC, the saluki is one of the oldest known dog breeds. The saluki was an important dog in **ancient** Egypt, where it was highly respected. It was known as *el hor* or "the noble one." Images of salukis have been found in paintings and on carvings and pottery across Egypt, Asia, and parts of Europe.

Salukis generally have smooth fur, with longer, fluffier fur on the ears and tail. They are built tall and lean. Males can reach 28 inches (71.1 cm) tall, and generally weigh about 50 pounds (22.6 kg). Originally a hunting dog, salukis run very fast and are always up for a chase.

**The saluki's long legs give the dog grace and speed while running.**

**1** Begin by drawing three circles. Notice where they are placed on the page and their different sizes.

**2** Next, connect the circles to form the body of the saluki.

**3** Excellent! Now draw two shapes as shown to form the front and back legs of the saluki.

**4** Now finish the back legs by drawing in two curved lines as shown.

**5** Draw in the shape of the mouth in the front and the tail in the back. Notice how the tail falls between the two back legs.

**6** You're doing great! Now let's draw in the face. Draw an ear, an eye, the nose, and the mouth.

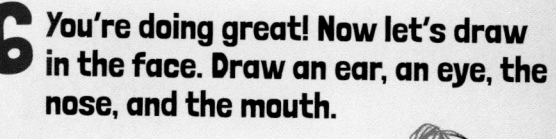

**7** Now if you'd like, draw in the coat of the saluki by shading your drawing as shown. To make the soft look of the coat, shade line by line. Wonderful! You just drew one of the oldest dog breeds, the saluki!

**21**

# DRAWING TERMS

There are some words and shapes you
will need to know to draw dogs.

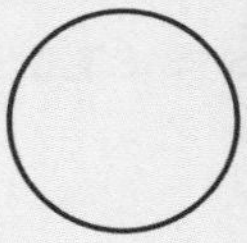

circle

curved line

rectangle

square

triangle

vertical line

wavy line

shading

# GLOSSARY

**ancestor:** A relative who lived long ago.

**ancient:** Very old; from a long time ago.

**breed:** A group of animals that look alike and have the same kind of relatives.

**develop:** To grow.

**evolve:** To develop and change over many years.

**loyal:** Supporting someone or taking their side.

**personality:** How a person or animal acts in relation to others.

**service animal:** An animal, most commonly a dog, that is trained to do work or perform tasks for the benefit of an individual with a disability.

**sniff:** Take in air through the nose.

**trait:** A feature that makes an individual special.

**unique:** One of a kind.

**yodel:** To make a sound by changing from a natural voice to one much higher in pitch, and quickly back again.

# INDEX

# WEBSITES

Due to the changing nature of Internet links, PowerKids Press has developed an online list of websites related to the subject of this book. This site is updated regularly. Please use this link to access the list:
www.powerkidslinks.com/ltd/dogs